SOCRATES

Anthony Gottlieb

DEER PARK PUBLIC LIBRARY
44 LAKE AVENUE
DEER PARK, NY 11729

ROUTLEDGE
New York

Published in 1999 by
Routledge
29 West 35th Street
New York, NY 10001

First published in 1997 by
Phoenix
A Division of the Orion Publishing Group Ltd.
Orion House
5 Upper Saint Martin's Lane
London WC2H 9EA

Copyright © 1999 by Anthony Gottlieb.
Printed in the United States of America on acid-free paper.

All rights reserved. No part of this book may be reprinted or
reproduced or utilized in any form or by any electronic, mechanical,
other means, now or hereafter invented, including photocopying
and recording or in any information storage or retrieval system,
without permission in writing from the publisher.

10 9 8 7 6 5 4 3 2 1

Library of Congress Cataloging-in-Publication Data

Gottlieb, Anthony.
        Socrates / Anthony Gottlieb.
         p. cm.—(The great philosophers : 6)
        Includes bibliographical references.
        ISBN 0-415-92381-6 (pbk.)
        1. Socrates. I. Title. II. Series: Great Philosophers
        (Routledge (Firm)) : 6.
B317.G68 1999
183'.2—dc21   99-22486
                                                    CIP

The author is grateful to Sir Kenneth Dover for his comments on a draft of this work.

This text is part of a forthcoming history of western philosophy, to be published by Viking / Penguin.

SOCRATES

Philosophy's Martyr

PHILOSOPHY'S MARTYR: SOCRATES

Socrates is the saint and martyr of philosophy. No other great philosopher has been so obsessed with righteous living. Like many martyrs, Socrates chose not to try to save his life when he probably could have done so by changing his ways. According to Plato, who was there at the time, Socrates told the judges at his trial that '[y]ou are mistaken ... if you think that a man who is worth anything ought to spend his time weighing up the prospects of life and death. He has only one thing to consider in performing any action – that is, whether he is acting rightly or wrongly.' But, unlike many saints, Socrates had a lively sense of humour; this sometimes appeared as playful wit, sometimes as pregnant irony. And, unlike the saints of any and every religion, his faith consisted not in a reliance on revelation or blind hope but in a devotion to argumentative reason. He would not be swayed by anything less.

His friends told stories about how strange he was. After dinner one night, according to a dialogue of Plato's, a young man who had been on military service with Socrates recounted how Socrates had

> started wrestling with some problem or other about sunrise one morning, and stood there lost in thought, and when the answer wouldn't come he still stood there thinking and refused to give it up. Time went on, and by about midday the troops ... began telling each other

how Socrates had been standing there thinking ever since daybreak. And at last, toward nightfall, some of the Ionians brought out their bedding after supper ... partly to see whether he was going to stay there all night. Well, there he stood till morning, and then at sunrise he said his prayers to the sun and went away.

Despite such uses of his spare time, Socrates had by all accounts an honourable military record.

Another friend described how, on the way to the dinner party at which the above story is told, Socrates 'fell into a fit of abstraction and began to lag behind'. Socrates then lurked in a neighbour's porch to continue thinking. 'It's quite a habit of his, you know; off he goes and there he stands, no matter where it is.' His other regular habits did not include washing; even his best friends admitted that it was unusual to see him freshly bathed and with his shoes on. He was shabby and unkempt, never had any money or cared where his next meal was coming from. He admitted to the court that 'I have never lived an ordinary quiet life. I did not care for the things that most people care about – making money, having a comfortable home, high military or civil rank, and all the other activities ... which go on in our city.' But Socrates did not think that any of these trappings of a conventionally successful life were bad in themselves. Neither was he an ascetic in the ordinary sense of the term. He never preached abstinence (he could, said his friends, drink any of them under the table, though he was never seen to be drunk), nor did he urge others to live as simply as he did. A hardy and pre-occupied man, he was just too busy to pay much attention to such things as clothing, food or money.

For most of the time he was busy talking to others, not just contemplating by himself. His discussions, it seems, were as intense as his fits of solitary abstraction. A distinguished general who knew him once said:

> anyone who is close to Socrates and enters into conversation with him is liable to be drawn into an argument, and whatever subject he may start, he will be continually carried round and round by him, until at last he finds that he has to give an account both of his present and past life, and when he is once entangled, Socrates will not let him go until he has completely and thoroughly sifted him.

Socrates was poor, had no conventional achievements to his name and was of humble birth – his father was a stonemason and his mother was a midwife. The fact that he nevertheless had an entrée to Athenian high society attests to his remarkable conversation. Alcibiades, who told the story of Socrates' vigil at camp, compared his speech to the music of Marsyas, the river god 'who had only to put his flute to his lips to bewitch mankind'. The 'difference between you and Marsyas,' Alcibiades tells Socrates, 'is that you can get just the same effect without any instrument at all – with nothing but a few simple words, not even poetry.' And:

> speaking for myself, gentlemen, if I wasn't afraid you'd tell me I was completely bottled, I'd swear on oath what an extraordinary effect his words have had on me ... For the moment I hear him speak I am smitten with a kind of

sacred rage ... and my heart jumps into my mouth and the tears start into my eyes – oh, and not only me, but lots of other men ...

This latter-day Marsyas, here, has often left me in such a state of mind that I've felt I simply couldn't go on living the way I did ... He makes me admit that while I'm spending my time on politics I am neglecting all the things that are crying for attention in myself.

The young Alcibiades was indeed 'bottled' at this stage of the dinner, so no doubt he was getting carried away. It is a telling fact that everyone got carried away when they talked about Socrates, whether it was Alcidiades singing his praises or his enemies ranting against him.

Alcibiades also wanted Socrates to love him. It was fairly usual for dealings between Athenian philosphers and young men to be tinged with homo-eroticism, especially among Plato's circle. Attracted by the youthful beauty of boys, an older man would happily hold their attention by spooning them wisdom. But both Plato and Socrates criticized homosexual intercourse; Alcibiades had at first been mortified when Socrates refused to return his physical affections. As Socrates had tactfully explained at the time, he resisted the advances of Alcibiades for ethical reasons, not because he was not attracted to him. Alcibiades was famously handsome and Socrates was famously ugly. It was an inner beauty that Alcibiades saw in him: 'I've been bitten in the heart, or the mind, or whatever you like to call it, by Socrates' philosophy, which clings like an adder to any young and gifted mind it can get hold of.'

Socrates poked fun at his own ugliness, and he could

make something more than half-serious out of even such a lighthearted subject as that. Critobulus, a friend of Socrates, apparently once challenged him to a 'beauty contest' in which each man was to try to convince a mock jury that he was better looking than the other. Socrates begins the contest:

Socrates The first step, then, in my suit, is to summon you to the preliminary hearing; be so kind as to answer my questions ... Do you hold ... that beauty is to be found only in man, or is it also in other objects?

Critobulus In faith, my opinion is that beauty is to be found quite as well in a horse or an ox or in any number of inanimate things. I know, at any rate, that a shield may be beautiful, or a sword, or a spear.

Soc. How can it be that all these things are beautiful when they are entirely dissimilar?

Crit. Why, they are beautiful and fine if they are well made for the respective functions for which we obtain them or if they are naturally well constituted to serve our needs.

Soc. Do you know the reason why we need eyes?

Crit. Obviously to see with.

Soc. In that case it would appear without further ado that my eyes are finer ones than yours.

Crit. How so?

Soc. Because, while yours see only straight ahead, mine, by bulging out as they do, see also to the sides.

Crit. Do you mean to say that a crab is better equipped visually than any other creature?

Soc. Absolutely ...

Crit. Well, let that pass; but whose nose is finer, yours or mine?

Soc. Mine, I consider, granting that Providence made us noses to smell with. For your nostrils look down toward the ground, but mine are wide open and turned outward so that I can catch scents from all about.

Crit. But how do you make a snub nose handsomer than a straight one?

Soc. For the reason that it does not put a barricade between the eyes but allows them unobstructed vision of whatever they desire to see; whereas a high nose, as if in despite, has walled the eyes off one from the other.

Crit. As for the mouth, I concede that point. For if it is created for the purpose of biting off food, you could bite off a far bigger mouthful than I could. And don't you think that your kiss is also the more tender because you have thick lips?

Soc. According to your argument, it would seem that I have a mouth more ugly even than an ass's ...

Crit. I cannot argue any longer with you, let them distribute the ballots ...

Of course Socrates lost. He knew he could not really be said to be good-looking, and they were only having fun. This exchange (from a dialogue by another admirer, Xenophon) is not the sort of thing that would bring tears to the eyes of Alcibiades, unless perhaps they were tears of laughter. Nor yet does it show Socrates at his most sophisticated. Far from it: this is the Beginner's Socrates. But it is interesting to see how this simple banter has much of the Socrates that one meets in the weightier and better-known philosophical exchanges in Plato's dialogues.

First there is his characteristic method of interrogation.

Instead of proposing a thesis himself, Socrates lets the other man do so and then draws out its consequences. As always with Socrates, the business begins with a request for an enlightening definition of whatever is being discussed – in this case, of beauty. Critobulus takes the bait and offers as his definition: '[things are] beautiful and fine if they are well made for the respective functions for which we obtain them or if they are naturally well consituted to serve our needs'. Then Socrates reels him in. He has no difficulty in showing that if this is what beauty is, then he himself is beautiful. Unravelling the accounts of others is how Socrates always played the game of dialectic.

The contest also shows Socrates' complex irony. He knows that he is ugly. He knows that Critobulus' definition of beauty is faulty. Yet he proceeds as if neither of these things were so: he seems perfectly happy to adopt the definition and to use it to prove that he is in fact good-looking. But he is not just trying to exploit Critobulus' words to win the beauty contest by foul means. He is not really trying to win it at all. While pretending to fight the contest, Socrates is in fact doing something else. By playfully adopting Critobulus' definition, Socrates demonstrates that Critobulus has failed to get to the bottom of what beauty is. It cannot be defined in terms of fitness and usefulness alone, since this would imply that Socrates' features are beautiful, which everybody knows they are not. Thus, while ironically pretending to convince Critobulus of his beauty, Socrates has in fact established the negative result that beauty cannot be what Critobulus says it is.

Socrates frequently and tiresomely denied that he knew anything about beauty or virtue or justice, or whatever else was being discussed. Such avowed ignorance was his trademark. Like his playful claim to personal beauty, these denials were partly ironic, though with a more serious purpose. Although he always claimed to have nothing to teach, his activities looked very much like teaching – enough so to get him hauled before the courts as a teacher with a malign influence. I shall now turn to the trial of Socrates and his defence, which show just what it was that made him so unpopular with some conservative Athenians, and so popular with most subsequent philosophers.

The trial of Socrates took place in 399 BC when he was nearly seventy. The charges were that he refused to recognize the official gods of the state, that he introduced new gods and that he corrupted the young. There was a vivid political background to the trial, but this does not mean that the charges were a sham and that the trial was really a political one. Politics, religion and education were all intertwined in the matter, and, however you looked at it, Socrates was saying the wrong things at the wrong time.

In 404 BC, five years before the trial, a twenty-seven-year war between Athens and Sparta had ended with the defeat of Athens. The Athenian democracy was overthrown and replaced by a group of men, subsequently known as the Thirty Tyrants, who were installed by Sparta. In the course of earning their name, the Tyrants murdered so many people that they lasted for only a year, though it was not until 401 BC that democracy was fully restored. Understandably, the democrats were still feeling rather insecure in 399 BC.

There were plenty of reasons to be uneasy about the presence of Socrates in the city.

Two close former associates of his had been involved in the tyranny. One, Critias, was the leader of the Thirty and a particularly bloodthirsty man. The other, Charmides, was one of their deputies (both men were, incidentally, relations of Plato's). Alcibiades had also turned out to be rather a liability. A headstrong and arrogant aristocrat, he was accused of sacrilegious high-jinks and profanity – committed, perhaps, while 'bottled'. Alcibiades heard about these charges while he was on a military expedition to Sicily. Rather than return to face them, he defected and treacherously fought on the side of Sparta instead. None of this looked good for these men's former mentor, Socrates.

In 403 BC, however, a political amnesty had been declared in Athens, so it would not have been possible to indict Socrates on explicitly political charges, even if anyone had wanted to. Besides, there were deeper causes for concern about his influence. During the long war with Sparta, Athenians had grown increasingly nervous about the home front. It was felt that intellectuals were weakening Athenian society by undermining its traditional views and values. Well might a man who captivated idle youths with his questioning about justice have aroused suspicion. The fact that there had been a hilarious caricature of Socrates as a bumbling but subversive teacher in a play by Aristophanes, staged in Athens twenty-four years earlier, did not help matters. And whatever truth there was to the rumour that Socrates disbelieved in the traditional gods – he seemed to deny the charge, but not convincingly – there was no doubt that he had an unorthodox approach to divinity. The way he talked about his *daimonion*, his 'guardian spirit' or personal 'divine sign', gave reasonable cause for concern that he did indeed 'introduce new gods', as the indictment put it. That would have been a grievous sin against the shaky democracy. The state alone had the power to say what was a suitable object for religious veneration; it had its own procedures for officially recognizing gods, and anyone who ignored them was in effect challenging the legitimacy of the democratic state. All of this Socrates was up against when he faced the 500 Athenian citizens who were to judge him.

Plato was at the trial; the *Apology* (or 'defence-speech') *of Socrates* which he wrote a few years afterwards was probably his first work. There are reasons to believe that in this work Plato tried harder to represent the real Socrates than he subsequently did elsewhere, though he did not necessarily try to reproduce his exact words. So I shall rely on Plato (as I have done for much of the information about Socrates provided so far). There is no alternative. The Socrates of Plato's *Apology* is the only Socrates there is, or has been for nearly all of the history of philosophy.

From a legal point of view, Socrates' speech is a miserable performance. He begins by saying that he has no skill as a speaker; this is a standard rhetorical first move, but in this case one would have to agree with him, if his aim in speaking were simply to get himself acquitted. Almost everything he says to rebut the official charges is either irrelevant or else unpersuasive. For example, on the subject of religion he confines himself to mocking his accuser. He gets him to contradict himself by provoking him into saying that Socrates is a complete atheist who believes in no gods at all. But if that were so, Socrates points out, how could he also be guilty of introducing new gods? To the charge that he has corrupted the young, Socrates makes the unconvincingly convoluted reply that he cannot intentionally have done any such thing, since this would have been against his own interests. To corrupt someone is to harm him, he says, and if you harm someone then that person will try to harm you back. So clearly he would not have risked that. This argument will have persuaded nobody.

Socrates knew that his judges were already prejudiced against him by the slanders of Aristophanes, and set out to correct these false impressions. He is not, he says, a man who teaches for money, like the professional 'Sophists' with whom Aristophanes has confused him. This seems to have been true enough: he did not charge a fee. But he did sing for his supper. He accepted hospitality in a tacit bargain for his edifying conversation, and apparently did no other sort of work. So the way he earned his living was not really different from that of the Sophists – not that either way of life would be regarded as inherently suspicious today. He also tried to dismiss the slander that he taught people how to win arguments by trickery when they were in the wrong. Far from it, he protested, for he did not know enough to teach anybody anything.

This is the main theme of the *Apology*, which is more of a general defence of his way of life than a rebuttal of the official charges. The nub of this defence is Socrates' claim that he has positively benefited the Athenians by subjecting them to his philosophical cross-examinations, but that they have failed to realize this and merely been angered by it, which is why he has ended up on trial for his life.

Socrates says that he is fulfilling the wishes of the gods when he goes about and argues with people. A friend of his once went to the oracle at Delphi and asked if there was any man wiser than Socrates. No, came back the answer, which threw Socrates into a frightful confusion – or so he says. For he always held that he was not wise at all. 'After puzzling about it for some time, I set myself at last with considerable reluctance to check the truth of it.' He did so by interrogating all sorts of people who had a reputation for wisdom or specialized knowledge. But he was always disappointed, because it seemed that there was nobody whose alleged wisdom could stand up to his questioning. He was always able to refute the efforts of others to establish some thesis of theirs, usually by highlighting some unwelcome and unexpected consequences of their views. He also questioned poets, but they could not even elucidate their poems to his satisfaction. After one such encounter:

> I reflected as I walked away, Well, I am certainly wiser than this man. It is only too likely that neither of us has any knowledge to boast of, but he thinks that he knows something which he does not know, whereas I am quite conscious of my ignorance. At any rate it seems that I am wiser than he is to this small extent, that I do not think that I know what I do not know.

Then it dawned on him what the oracle must have meant:

> whenever I succeed in disproving another person's claim to wisdom in a given subject, the bystanders assume that I know everything about that subject myself. But the truth of the matter, gentleman, is pretty certainly this,

that real wisdom is the property of God, and this oracle is his way of telling us that human wisdom has little or no value. It seems to me that he is not referring to Socrates, but has merely taken my name as an example, as if he would say to us, The wisest of you men is he who has realized, like Socrates, that in respect of wisdom, he is really worthless.

In other words, the superior wisdom of Socrates lies in the fact that he alone is aware of how little he knows. Of course, there is a little more to Socrates' wisdom than just that, as he is made to admit elsewhere in Plato's dialogues. Although, he claims, 'the arguments never come out of me; they always come from the person I am talking with', he acknowledges that he is 'at a slight advantage in having the skill to get some account of the matter from another's wisdom and entertain it with fair treatment'. He aptly describes himself as an intellectual midwife, whose questioning delivers the thoughts of others into the light of day. But this skill in elucidation and debate, which he obviously has in abundance, is not a form of real wisdom so far as Socrates is concerned. Real wisdom is perfect knowledge about ethical subjects, about how to live. When Socrates claims ignorance, he means ignorance about the foundations of morality; he is not asserting any general sort of scepticism about everyday matters of fact. His concern is solely with ethical reflection, and he cannot with a clear conscience abandon his mission to encourage it in others:

> If I say that this would be disobedience to God, and that is why I cannot 'mind my own business', you will not believe that I am serious. If on the other hand I tell you

that to let no day pass without discussing goodness and all other subjects about which you hear me talking and examining both myself and others is really the very best thing that a man can do, and that life without this sort of examination is not worth living, you will be even less inclined to believe me. Nevertheless that is how it is.

His pious references to the wisdom of God (sometimes he speaks of a single God, sometimes of the gods) are apt to disguise how unconventional his attitude to divinity was. When he says that only God has wisdom, he seems to mean this figuratively, just as one might shrug and say, 'God knows!'. For consider how he sets about interpreting 'God's' words and trying to tease out hints of 'His' wisdom. The Delphic oracle was as authentic a voice of God as any available: yet Socrates did not just accept what it says but instead set out 'to check the truth of it'. He says elsewhere that 'it has always been my nature never to accept advice from any of my friends unless reflection shows that it is the best course that reason offers; he seems to have adopted exactly the same approach to the advice of God. Presented with the divine pronouncement that no man is wiser than Socrates, he refuses to take this at face value until he has satisfied himself that a true meaning can be found for it.

He seems to be speaking in a roundabout way when he refers to his mission as divine, because the Delphic oracle did not explicitly tell him to go forth and philosophize. He does at one point say that his mission to argue and question was undertaken 'in obedience to God's commands given in oracles and dreams and in every other way that any divine dispensation has ever impressed a duty upon man'. But when he continues by saying that this is a true statement 'and easy to verify', his verification consists merely in arguing that his mission is a morally good thing. He does not give any evidence that God told him to do it. He probably came closest to the heart of the matter when he said, 'I want you to think of my adventures as a sort of pilgrimage undertaken to establish the truth of the oracle once for all.' It was his conscience and intelligence which told him to interrogate those who believed themselves to be wise. He could claim that this 'helps the cause of God' because such activities do help to confirm the Delphic pronouncement that nobody is wiser than Socrates. But the talk of God is largely a gloss, which serves to mark Socrates' high moral purpose and to win the approval of his hearers. His basic motive for philosophizing was simply that it seemed to him the right thing to do.

Socrates says he is influenced in his actions by what he calls his *daimonion*, a guardian spirit or voice which has been with him since childhood. This seems to have been the unorthodox divinity or 'new gods' referred to in the charges against him. Once again the advice of the *daimonion* is treated as advice to be reasoned with before it is endorsed, like the counsel of friends or the words of the Delphic oracle. The voice of the *daimonion* is pretty clearly what we would call the voice of cautious conscience. He says that 'when it comes it always dissuades me from what I am proposing to do, and never urges me on'.

The guardian spirit warned him off any involvement in politics, he says, because if he had made a public figure of himself, he would have been killed long before he could have done much good. That is why he chose to minister to the people privately:

> I spend all my time going about trying to persuade you, young and old, to make your first and chief concern not for your bodies nor for your possessions, but for the highest welfare of your souls, proclaiming as I go, wealth does not bring goodness, but goodness brings wealth and every other blessing, both to the individual and to the state.

This persuasion seems to have been rather strident at times. He implies that the Athenians should be 'ashamed that you give your attention to acquiring as much money as possible, and similarly with reputation and honour, and give no attention or thought to truth and understanding and the perfection of your soul'. He must have particularly annoyed them when he said, during his trial, that he thought he was doing the Athenians 'the greatest possible service' in showing them the errors of their ways. This was at a stage of the proceedings when he had already been voted guilty and was required to argue for a suitable penalty, to counter the prosecution's proposal that he be put to death. Typically, he treats this responsibility with irony. What he actually deserves for doing the Athenians such a service, he says, is not a punishment but a reward. He suggests free meals for life at the expense of the state. Such an honour was usually reserved for victors at the Olympic games and suchlike; he has earned it even more than they have, he says, because 'these people give you the semblance of success, but I give you the reality'. He ends this part of the speech by suggesting a fine instead, at the instigation of Plato and other friends who offer to pay it for him. But the Athenians had already lost their patience. They voted for the death penalty by a larger majority than that by which they had found him guilty. This means that some of them, having previously found him innocent, were so enraged by his cheek that they either changed their minds or else decided to get rid of him anyway.

One story has it that as Socrates was leaving the court, a devoted but dim admirer called Apollodorus moaned that the hardest thing for him to bear was that Socrates was being put to death unjustly. What? said Socrates, trying to comfort him. Would you rather I was put to death justly?

As for the prospect of death itself, he was already very old and close to death anyway, so he says, and he had had a good and useful life. Besides:

> to be afraid of death is only another form of thinking that one is wise when one is not ... No one knows with regard to death whether it is really the greatest blessing that can happen to a man, but people dread it as though they were certain that it is the greatest evil, and this ignorance, which thinks that it knows what it does not, must surely be ignorance most culpable ... and if I were to claim to be wiser than my neighbour in any respect, it would be in this ... that not possessing any real knowledge of what comes after death, I am also conscious that I do not possess it.

If there were an afterlife, he added, he would get the chance to meet 'heroes of the old days who met their death through an unfair trial, and to compare my fortunes with theirs – it would be rather amusing'.

For all his talk of ignorance, and his insistence that he merely acted as a midwife for the ideas of others, Socrates did have strong beliefs of his own. Unfortunately he never wrote them down. For one of these beliefs was that philosophy is an intimate and collaborative activity; it is a matter for discussions among small groups of people who argue together in order that each might find the truth for himself. The spirit of such a pastime cannot accurately be captured in a lecture or a treatise. That is one reason why Plato and Xenophon (and several of their contemporaries whose works are now lost) chose to present Socrates' teaching in the form of dialogues. Dialogue had been his *métier* and dialogue would be his monument.

There are four main witnesses for the intimate thoughts of Socrates: Plato, Xenophon, Aristophanes and Aristotle. None of these men is quite what a historian might have wished for. Plato has by far the most to say on the subject, but as an objective guide to Socrates he suffers from the disability of having practically worshipped him. He is therefore likely to have exaggerated what he took to be his finest qualities. Also, in the course of some forty years of thinking and teaching, during which Plato's ideas naturally changed quite a lot, he paid Socrates the tribute of using him as a mouthpiece. To Plato, Socrates was pre-eminently wise, so whenever something seemed to Plato to be wise, he put it in the mouth of Socrates. Plato himself – or else a close associate – once described his dialogues as 'the work of a Socrates embellished and modernized'. This is double trouble, because not only does the Socrates in Plato's dialogues often speak for Plato rather than for himself, but he is also made to say rather different things at the various stages of Plato's literary career.

What about the other three witnesses? Xenophon's failings as a source are quite different. He was not (like Plato) too much of a philosopher to act as a guide to Socrates, but rather too little of one. It is no crime to be a retired general turned gentleman-farmer, but such a man is perhaps not the safest custodian of the key to one of the world's great thinkers. Xenophon implausibly uses the figure of Socrates to pass on his own tips about farming and military tactics. He also depicts him as a boringly conventional goody-goody: 'All his private conduct was lawful and helpful: to public authority he rendered such scrupulous obedience in all that the laws required, both in civil life and in military service, that he was a pattern of good discipline to all.' A leading scholar of ancient philosophy has understandably referred to Xenophon as 'that stuffy old prig'. In fairness to Xenophon it must be said that anyone who admired an eccentric like Socrates as much as he did cannot have been all that stuffy. But Xenophon was certainly no Socrates himself, and he may often have failed to grasp both the strangeness of his character and what he was getting at. If Xenophon tried too hard to make Socrates respectable and a sound chap, then the playwright Aristophanes tried too hard to do the opposite. His Socrates is a slapstick fool who is intrigued by such questions as from which end a gnat breaks wind. Aristotle's disability in describing Socrates is simply stated: he was born fifteen years too late.

Yet it is Aristotle who holds a vital clue. Although he never heard Socrates' opinions at first hand, he studied for some twenty years in Plato's Academy and had plenty of opportunity to hear Plato's views from Plato himself. He was therefore in a position to disentangle the thinking of the two men. To a considerable extent, Aristotle's testimony lets one subtract Plato from his own dialogues and see the Socratic remainder. Aristotle was also much less in awe of Socrates than Plato was, and therefore managed to take a more dispassionate approach to his teachings.

The fact that the four main sources for Socrates were so different turns out to be something of a boon. It means that the features which are common to their various accounts are all the more likely to be authentic. And the more we know about each of the four and what he was up to, the easier it is to discount his bias and see the true Socrates loitering behind. By following up such clues, modern scholars have pieced together much of the philosophy of the man who literally argued himself to death.

It is simplest to consider the views of Socrates in relation to those of Plato. The approximate dating of Plato's dialogues, plus some information about his life, make it possible to retrace his steps on an intellectual journey that started in the company of Socrates but eventually left him far behind. At first Plato largely limited himself to recreating the conversations of his revered teacher. Gradually, Pythagorean and other mystical glosses were put on Socrates' ideas as Plato came increasingly under the influence of Italian Pythagoreans. And eventually Plato reached a point where he invoked the name of Socrates to expound on all sorts of subjects.

The important discussions of the real Socrates were exclusively concerned with how one ought to live. They were mostly about the virtues, of which there were conventionally held to be five: courage, moderation, piety, wisdom and justice. His mission was to urge people to care for their souls by trying to understand and acquire these qualities. This task was enough to keep Socrates busy, but Plato was much more ambitious on his master's behalf. He wrote many dialogues that do not focus on morality at all but which usually still have Socrates as the main speaker. For example, Plato's *Republic* starts out as a discussion of justice but ends up touching on practically everything that interested Plato.

Even when the real Socrates made a point of saying that he did not have a clue, Plato often plunged ahead and credited him with firm opinions. For instance, Socrates thought that what happens after death is an open question. But in the *Phaedo*, which purports to give Socrates' last words before he drank hemlock in prison, Plato makes him produce a whole barrage of proofs for the immortality of the soul.

Plato seems to have had few doubts about what would happen after death. He thought that the soul was separable from the body, that it existed before birth and that it would definitely continue to exist after death. Under Pythagorean influence, he held that while it was tied to a physical body during life it led a defiled and inferior existence from which it needed to be 'purified' and 'freed from the shackles of the body'. According to Plato in this dialogue, what the good man can hope to enjoy after death is reunification, or at least communion, with those incorporeal higher forms of existence that are conventionally called 'the divine'. The philosopher, in particular, should regard the whole of his life as a preparation for the blissful release of death. As we have seen, Socrates lived a shambling, poor and unconventional life that was certainly unworldly. But Plato was positively other-worldly, which is a rather different thing (and actually he led a mostly comfortable existence until escaping the shackles of his amply fed body).

Socrates pursued the virtues because he felt morally obliged to, here and now. Earthly life imposed its own duties, brought its own blessings and was not simply a preparation for something else. Plato's motives were less straightforward because he had at least one eye fixed on something beyond. One belief about virtue that the two men held in common is that the pursuit of goodness is not only a matter of acting in certain ways but also an intellectual project. Yet they saw this project differently. Socrates believed that coming to understand the virtues was a necessary precondition for possessing them. A man could not be truly virtuous unless he knew what virtue was, and the only way he might be able to get this knowledge was by examining accounts of the particular virtues. That is why Socrates went around questioning people and arguing with them. Plato believed in this argumentative search too, but he also interpreted it as something almost mystical. While Socrates saw the search for definitions as a means to an end, namely the exercise of virtue, Plato saw the search as an end in itself. To look for a definition was, for Plato, to seek the ideal, eternal, unchanging Form of whatever was under discussion; the contemplation of such Forms was itself the highest good. That is what he thought Socrates' questioning really amounted to and what it ought to aim at.

For Plato, philosophy was the ladder to this elevated

world of the Forms, but not everyone could climb it. Its higher rungs were reserved for those who were especially talented in dialectical argument, an élite, like the initiates of cult religions, or the followers of Pythagoras who had been privy to the master's secrets. Socrates had a more egalitarian approach to knowledge and virtue. The unexamined life, as he famously said in his defence-speech, is not worth living, and this is not a fate to which he meant to condemn all but a chosen few. Anybody could examine his own life and ideas and thus lead a worthwhile existence. Socrates would happily question and argue with anybody, cobbler or king, and for him this was all that philosophy was. He would have had little use for Plato's Forms or the rare skills needed to find them.

One thing which led Plato to the mysterious Forms was his fascination with mathematics, again a Pythagorean matter and again a point of difference between him and Socrates. Above its gates, Plato's Academy was said to have had the words 'No one ignorant of geometry admitted here'; Aristotle later complained that for Plato's followers, 'mathematics has come to be the whole of philosophy' – a petulant exaggeration, but a pointed one. What struck Plato about the objects dealt with in mathematics, such as numbers and triangles, is that they are ideal, eternal, unchanging and pleasingly independent of earthly, visible things. Plainly one cannot see or touch the number four: it therefore exists in a different sort of realm, according to Plato. And the lines, triangles and other sorts of objects that figure in mathematical proofs cannot be identified with anything physical either. Particular physical lines and triangles are nothing more than approximations to ideal mathematical ones. A perfect line, for example, would have no thickness; but any visible line, or rim of a physical object, always will. Given the impressiveness of mathematics, Plato reasoned, other sorts of knowledge ought to copy it and be about ideal and incorporeal objects too. These objects of knowledge were the Forms.

In one of his dialogues, Plato used a geometrical example to argue that knowledge of the Forms, which for him meant all the important sorts of knowledge, is acquired before birth. The truths of pure reason, such as those of mathematics, are not discovered afresh but are painstakingly recollected from a previous existence in which the soul was disembodied and could encounter the Forms directly. Thus one does not strictly speaking learn these truths at all: one works to remember them. When a soul is born into a body, the knowledge which it previously enjoyed slips from memory: as Wordsworth wrote in his *Intimations of Immortality*, 'our birth is but a sleep and a forgetting'. Wordsworth was not particularly thinking about geometry, but he liked the general idea. To illustrate this theory, Plato makes 'Socrates' elicit some apparent knowledge of geometry from an uneducated slave-boy. This is supposed both to confirm the Platonic idea that some knowledge is recollected from an earlier existence and to show why the teaching of Socrates is indeed, as Socrates had claimed, really like midwifery.

The problem which 'Socrates' sets the slave is that of determining the sides of a square of a given area. He starts by drawing a square whose sides are two feet long, and whose area is thus four square feet, and asks how long the sides would have to be if its area were instead eight square feet. At first the slave ignorantly reasons that the sides would have to be twice as long as those of the original square, i.e., four feet. By drawing another diagram, 'Socrates' soon shows him that this must be wrong, since the area of such a square would be not eight but sixteen square feet. The slave is surprised to learn that he does not know as much as he thought he did. 'Socrates' notes that at this point, 'we have helped him to some extent toward finding the right answer, for now not only is he ignorant of it but he will be quite glad to look for it.' Next, with the aid of further diagrams and by asking the right questions about them, Socrates gradually leads the slave to work out the answer for himself: the sides of a triangle with twice the area of the original one would have to be the same length as a diagonal drawn across the original square – which, in effect, boils down to the famous theorem of Pythagoras. Bingo: since Socrates never actually told him this, the slave must have 'known' it already.

This little episode does not really prove Plato's theory of recollection, as Plato himself acknowledged. But the story does illustrate a distinctly Socratic thesis about knowledge and how it can be imparted. Socrates' questions to the slave are indeed leading ones (and the diagrams help, too), yet it is nevertheless true that the slave comes to see the answer for himself. He has not simply been told it as one might be told how many feet there are in a yard or what the capital of Greece is. He has come to appreciate something through his own intellectual faculties. So Socrates can modestly make his usual claim that he has not handed over any knowledge himself but has just acted as a midwife to bring it out of somebody else. And there is another thing: as

Socrates points out, in order for the slave to know this piece of mathematics properly, it is not quite enough for him to work through the example just once:

> At present these opinions [of the slave's], being newly aroused, have a dreamlike quality. But if the same questions are put to him on many occasions and in different ways, you can see that in the end he will have a knowledge on the subject as accurate as anybody's ...
>
> This knowledge will not come from teaching but from questioning. He will recover it for himself.

Repeated doses of Socratic questioning are called for. In other words, what the slave needs is exactly the sort of treatment that the real Socrates offered the largely ungrateful Athenians. As he says in the *Apology*, if anyone claims to know about goodness, 'I shall question him and examine him and test him.' Thus, in his fanciful story of assisted recollection, Plato has given us a striking illustration of the sort of thing Socrates was doing when he claimed to help other people deliver their own opinions. It is as if Socrates were drawing out and firming up some knowledge that was already there.

This is all very well for Plato's example of his beloved triangles and squares. It is not hard to believe that a skilled questioner can bring a pupil to appreciate a mathematical truth without explicitly stating this truth for him – anyone who has had a good teacher will recognize this experience. But what about matters of justice and the other virtues, which is what the real Socrates was interested in? Ethics is messier than mathematics; it does not, for one thing, seem to have any proofs to offer. So presumably the business of learning about virtue will be quite different from the business of learning about mathematics.

Socrates knew this. He had no illusions about being able conclusively to prove any ethical doctrines. Quite the contrary, in fact, for he was forever insisting on his own uncertainty and the tentativeness of his enquiries. For example, before starting a defence of one thesis, he admits that, 'Sometimes, however, I am of the opposite opinion, for I am all abroad in my ideas about this matter, a condition obviously occasioned by ignorance.' No doubt he is wrong to maintain this thesis now, he says to his interlocutor, but let us follow the argument wherever it leads and perhaps you will be able to put me right. When Socrates says earlier on in this dialogue that, 'I am full of defects, and always getting things wrong in some way or other', he is partly just being modest. But he was quite clear that he had no mathematical-style proofs about virtue.

Does he ever get anywhere, then? Does he really succeed in delivering any knowledge about virtue? In one sense, yes. He does, albeit indirectly, lay out several pronounced and rather extraordinary views about virtue, which all slot together to form a theory of human life. As for whether he succeeds in convincing his hearers of this theory, the answer is generally no. But he does not really aim to do that anyway because he is not absolutely sure that the theory is right and, besides, people must find their own way to the truth about such matters. What he aims to do is to put opinions about virtue to the test, and this applies both to his own opinions and to those of the people he is talking to. The test is to be trial by dialectical ordeal: definitions or accounts of various matters are to be queried and thereby elucidated, and whatever seems to survive such questioning is provisionally to be accepted. The results yielded by this approach fall short of true wisdom in various ways, but it is nevertheless the best approach available. Such enquiry does lead to a sort of knowledge, so Socrates' bare-faced denials that he knows anything are partly ironic.

Most of the authentically Socratic investigations in Plato's dialogues wind up without settling on a final conclusion. Socrates ambitiously sets off to find out what, say, justice is; he argues away for a while; and then usually has to go home apparently empty handed. But he is not really empty handed. The discussions usually succeed at least in showing up something important along the way. For example, in one early Platonic dialogue, Socrates quizzes a man called Euthyphro on the nature of piety or holiness. Although Socrates does not manage to establish exactly what piety is, he does manage to show something interesting about what it is not.

The two men meet outside the law courts, where Euthyphro is about to prosecute his own father for unintentionally (though perhaps culpably) causing the death of a slave who had himself murdered another slave. Socrates is surprised that Euthyphro should want to pursue such a case. Euthyphro insists that although his family think it impious for a son to prosecute his father as a murderer, he knows what he is about. His family are ignorant about what is holy, whereas he has 'an accurate knowledge of all that'. He therefore has no doubts about the rightness of his action. Socrates wonders at Euthyphro's confident wisdom and asks him to share it and tell him what holiness is. At first Euthyphro says that it is what the gods love. But

Socrates gets him to see that since the gods are commonly represented as having fierce disagreements, they presumably do not always love or approve the same things. This means that whether or not a god approves something cannot be the criterion of whether or not it is holy: one god might approve it and another not, in which case one would be none the wiser as to its holiness. So Socrates and Euthyphro amend the proposed definition and say that the holy is what all the gods agree in approving. But now a question occurs to Socrates: 'Is what is holy holy because the gods approve it, or do they approve it because it is holy?'

This is an excellent question, so good in fact that at first Euthyphro does not understand it. It comes down to this: would absolutely anything that the gods approved of count as holy, just because they approved of it, or are they bound to approve only of certain things, namely those which would count as holy whether they approved of them or not? Unfortunately Plato did not have the vocabulary to make this distinction absolutely clear. So when Socrates tries to explain it, his account gets tangled in irrelevant grammatical matters and is not altogether compelling. Yet Socrates does seem to have uncovered a dilemma about the relationship between religion and morality. If we ask the same sort of question about what is morally good instead of about what is holy, we can see that we are faced with a revealing choice: either goodness cannot be explained simply by reference to what the gods want, or else it is an empty tautology to say that the gods are good – in which case the praise of the gods would simply be a matter of power-worship. As Leibniz put it, at the start of the eighteenth century (by which time the gods had long ago dwindled to one God):

> Those who believe that God has established good and evil by an arbitrary decree ... deprive God of the designation *good*: for what cause could one have to praise him for what he does, if in doing something quite different he would have done equally well?

The Socrates in Plato's dialogue did not develop the argument that far. But he does appear to have seen that moral values cannot simply be derived from considerations about what the gods want, since to do so would rob the gods (or God) of any distinctively moral authority. Euthyphro apparently accepts the point, though later he wavers and hurries into court before he can be pinned down. Thus Socrates does succeed in making useful progress even though he does not finally settle the matter at hand.

Yet there is still something unconvincing about what Socrates says he is up to in arguments like this. Can his questioning, or indeed any sort of intellectual enterprise, really have the sort of practical benefits he claims? Even though he never professes to establish the whole truth about virtue, and although we can agree that he nevertheless manages to make some intellectual headway, it is hard to see how his interrogations can have the power with which he seems to credit them. The problem lies in his belief that discussing the virtues can lead one actually to become a better person. This is no casual aside: it is this very idea which Socrates invokes to justify subjecting people to his trying examinations. It is all for their own good, he thinks, not only because such discussions are worthwhile in themselves but mainly because having them is the only path to personal virtue. This sounds implausible, to say the least. Surely it is one thing to come to know that a principle of action is right and quite another to behave in accordance with it. Could not someone find out all sorts of things about virtue by talking to Socrates but still go off and be wicked? As we have seen, Critias, Charmides and maybe Alcibiades seem to have done just that.

Aristotle frequently attacked Socrates along these lines: 'We must not limit our enquiry to knowing what it [virtue] is, but extend it to how it is to be produced.' He accused Socrates of failing to distinguish between practical questions and theoretical ones:

> he thought all the virtues to be kinds of knowledge, so that to know justice and to be just came simultaneously ... Therefore he enquired what virtue is, not how or from what it arises. This approach is correct with regard to theoretical knowledge, for there is no other part of astronomy or physics or geometry except knowing and contemplating the nature of things which are the subjects of those sciences ... But the aim of the practical sciences is different ... For we do not wish to know what bravery is but to be brave, nor what justice is but to be just, just as we wish to be in health rather than to know what health is ...

Socrates had a sort of answer to this. He could have replied along the following lines: 'You are not being fair to me. The reason why Critias, Charmides and some other troublesome pupils failed to be virtuous is simply that they had not yet learned enough about virtue. If only we had got further in our discussions, these people would indeed have become just. Thus while I agree that we not only want to know what virtue is but want to be virtuous ourselves, my point is that if we really did know what it was, virtue would follow of its own accord. As I keep saying, I do not yet know what it is; so I cannot yet produce it in myself, let alone in others. That is precisely why we must keep on looking for it.'

The main point of this reply is fair enough. We cannot say that Socrates' claim about what his methods could achieve has been refuted: it has never yet been put to the test, because he has not yet found out what virtue is. But even so, why should anyone believe him when he says that full knowledge of virtue, if we ever managed to get it, would itself produce virtuous behaviour? It sounds an implausible hypothesis when we consider how weak-willed, selfish and short-sighted people often are. People frequently think that something is morally wrong and yet do it anyway. Why should we think they would be any different if only they knew more?

Aristotle reckoned that Socrates suffered from an over-simplified picture of human psychology: 'He is doing away with the irrational part of the soul, and is thereby doing away also both with passion and character.' Socrates saw human action and emotion in largely rational or intellectual terms; he ignored impulses and wilful irrationality. 'No one, he said, acts against what he believes best – people act so only by reason of ignorance.' This explains the exaggerated importance that Socrates attached to enquiries about virtue. If the only reason why people fail to do whatever is best is that they are ignorant, then the cure for immorality would indeed be more knowledge.

On this subject, Plato seems for once to have been more down to earth and realistic than Socrates. He recognized an 'irrational part of the soul' and saw it as often in conflict with the rational part. (In his more Pythagorean moments, he described this as a conflict between soul and body.) Producing virtue was thus for Plato not just a matter of imparting knowledge but of encouraging certain behaviour. In the utopian state described in his *Republic*, this involved careful training and discipline of the young and close attention to their early environment – even to the sort of music they listened to and the sort of stories they were allowed to hear.

Socrates himself evidently had no need of such training. He was by all accounts supremely disciplined and a master of rational self-control. Maybe that was the problem. Perhaps it explains why he seems to have had such impossibly high expectations for others and to have supposed that if only they really knew what justice was they would immediately become just themselves. It has been said of Socrates that 'in the strength of his character lay the weakness of his philosophy'. This is a neat formulation, but the ideas of Socrates had rather more coherence than it suggests. Besides, it must be said that his implausibly rationalistic account of psychology was not the only problem anyway. Even if some wise person were as disciplined as he was, and had somehow been born with the irrational part of his soul missing, it is hard to see how this would automatically make such a person morally good. Could not someone be as rational as Socrates, as wise as he sought to be, but also as bad as Milton's Satan, who knowingly embraced evil with the words, 'Evil, be thou my Good'? Not according to Socrates, who held (said Aristotle) that 'No one would choose evil knowing it to be such.' Not only did Socrates conveniently ignore impulsiveness and irrationality, he apparently declared that wilful immortality was simply impossible. He seems never to have met a fallen man, let alone a fallen angel.

Was he then just naive? Nietzsche wrote of the 'divine naiveté and sureness of the Socratic way of life', but what he seems to have had in mind is the clear-eyed focus of Socrates' vision, not any merely foolish innocence. Nietzsche thought long and hard about Socrates' habit of expressing himself in apparently naive propositions, and concluded that it was in fact 'wisdom full of pranks'. Nietzsche realized that it is important to bear in mind the circumstances in which Socrates conducted his discussions. Most of the paradoxical views that can be attributed to Socrates are based on things which he said to someone, or which he agreed to, for a distinctive purpose and in a distinctive context. He sought to teach – while denying that he taught at all – by teasing, cajoling and provoking. He tried to uncover the truth about things by playfully trying out various ideas on his hearers. And intellectual pranks were no small part of it. 'This was Socrates' Muse,' wrote Galen, a doctor and philosopher of the second century AD: 'to mingle seriousness with a portion of lightheartedness.'

One cannot excuse all the implausibilities in his views by saying that he did not really mean them. This might salvage an appearance of mundane common sense for

Socrates, but only at the cost of discarding almost everything he said. One can, though, often interpret Socrates better by bearing his unusual educational project in mind. I shall now piece together the theory of human life that lies behind Socrates' apparently naive and implausible pronouncements. What emerges is a set of ideas that have proved to be, at the very least, extremely fruitful, not only in edifying some of his immediate hearers but also in stimulating a great deal of subsequent moral philosophy.

Socrates' theory starts and ends with the soul; in the *Apology*, he says that the most important thing in life is to look to its welfare. The soul, he says elsewhere, is that which is 'mutilated by wrong actions and benefited by right ones'. He does not mean the actions of others, but those of oneself. To do good is to benefit one's own soul and to do wrong is to harm it. Since the soul's welfare is paramount, no other sort of harm is so important. Nothing that other people can do to you can harm you enough to cancel out the benefit you bestow on yourself by acting rightly. It follows that bad people ultimately harm only themselves: 'Nothing can harm a good man either in life or after death.'

Socrates therefore has no fear of the court which is trying him. He will not stoop to dishonourable behaviour in order to win acquittal, for 'the difficulty is not so much to escape death; the real difficulty is to escape from doing wrong, which is far more fleet of foot'. One reason why it is hard to stop evil catching up with you is that if someone tries to do you wrong, it is often tempting to try to get your own back on them. But since it is always wrong to do evil – which would harm your soul whatever your excuse for doing it might be – Socrates points out that one must never return evil for evil. In other words, one must turn the other cheek.

This conflicts with old Greek moral conventions, according to which it is acceptable to harm one's enemies, though not one's friends and especially not one's family. The rigorous ethics of Socrates removes such distinctions between people and enjoins a universal morality instead. One striking thing about it is that it does so by appealing to self-interest, not to the sort of altruistic feelings that are usually thought of as the main motive for moral behaviour. Doing good is a matter of looking after the part of yourself which matters most, namely your soul. This is not like ordinary selfishness, though, because the only way to achieve this sort of benefit for yourself is by acting justly and practising the other virtues too. It cannot be gained by greedily putting your own interests above those of other people, but only by putting moral self-improvement above any other motive. Neither does this unusual ethics rest on any hope of heavenly reward or fear of its opposite. The benefits of virtue are reaped more or less immediately, for 'to live well means the same thing as to live honourably' and 'the just [man] is happy and the unjust miserable'. In Socrates' view, happiness and virtue are linked, which is why it is in people's own interests to be moral.

This is particularly hard to swallow. For one unfair fact of life is that the wicked do sometimes seem to prosper, which rather darkens Socrates' sunny landscape. But to Socrates' mind, the successful care of the soul brings all sorts of good things that may not immediately be apparent. He argues that there are unexpected connections between some of the good things in life, and that happiness turns out to be a more complicated matter than one might at first think. It might seem that wicked people can enjoy all sorts of pleasures, but in fact there are some that they cannot enjoy, and these are important enough to cast doubt on the idea that such people can truly be said to be happy at all. Intellectual pleasures allegedly come into this class, and there are all sorts of other satisfactions which cannot be obtained without the exercise of the virtues. To take a simple example: unless you practice the virtue of moderation, you will not enjoy good health, and will probably deprive yourself of many future pleasures for the sake of a few present ones. So without exercising the virtues a man cannot be all that happy after all.

It turns out that among the aspects of the good life which are subtly and surprisingly linked are the virtues themselves. Socrates argues that they come as a package-deal or not at all. His arguments typically proceed by trying to show that some particular virtue cannot work properly unless another is present as well. Courage, for instance, requires wisdom. It is no good being daring if you are foolish, for such would-be courage will degenerate into mere rashness. And all the other virtues are intertwined in similar ways. One of them, namely the virtue of wisdom, plays a special part. For without some degree of wisdom, people will be too bad at seeing the consequences of actions to be able to tell what is right and what is wrong, which is the fundamental prerequisite for virtuous living. Without wisdom they will be unable to be truly happy either, because every benefit that has the potential to make one happy also has the potential to be misused and thus to do the opposite. One therefore needs wisdom both to reap the benefits of good things and to be virtuous.

For Socrates, the connection between virtue and wisdom was so close that he seems in some sense to have identified the two. They certainly seemed to run into one another. According to Socrates, if someone has any of the other virtues, he must have wisdom as well – because otherwise he would not have managed to be virtuous. And if he has wisdom, he must have all of the virtues – because, being wise, he will realize that he cannot be happy without practising all the other virtues too. As we have seen, Socrates thought that moral behaviour benefits the soul and that a person who acts wickedly is doing himself a spiritual mischief. If this is true, then anyone who is genuinely wise will realize this fact. Anyone who realizes it – and who values his own soul, as any wise person surely must – will therefore try to avoid doing wrong. This train of thought explains why Socrates held that nobody does evil knowingly, for if someone does wrong, the only plausible explanation for his doing so is that he does not realize that his actions will harm his soul. He is, in effect, acting out of ignorance. All in all, these sorts of considerations supported Socrates' idea that if his discussions helped people towards wisdom, he would thereby be helping them towards virtue too.

In one of Plato's dialogues, Socrates encapsulates much of his theory in the course of summing up a discussion with Callicles, a young aristocrat who was about to enter public life:

So there is every necessity, Callicles, that the sound-minded and temperate man, being, as we have demonstrated, just and brave and pious, must be completely good, and the good man must do well and finely whatever he does, and he who does well must be happy and blessed, while the evil man who does ill must be wretched.

Did Socrates really manage to demonstrate all of that? His hearers frequently shied at the logical jumps he effortlessly made himself. So much seemed questionable, particularly what he said about happiness. Aristotle was typically forthright in his objections on this point: 'Those who say that the victim on the rack or the man who falls into great misfortunes is happy if he is good, are, whether they mean to or not, talking nonsense.' At one point one of Socrates' hearers understandably remarked, in no doubt baffled tones, that 'if you are serious and what you say is true, then surely the life of us mortals must be turned upside down'.

That is precisely what Socrates aimed to do: to reshape people's moral ideas. Clearly this was not going to be easy. In order to succeed in doing it by debate, the discussions would have to be rather different from purely theoretical ones, for 'it is no ordinary matter that we are discussing, but how we ought to live'. A degree of exaggereration and simplification would sometimes be needed if the ethical point at hand was to be made forcefully. For example, when Socrates said that nothing can harm a good man, he did not mean to deny that various undesirable things can happen to the virtuous. He was trying to persuade his hearers to regard such misfortunes as less important than the misfortune of spoiling your own soul. When he said

41

that the evil man is wretched, he did not mean that such a man could not occasionally enjoy a good night out. He was exhorting his hearers to appreciate the satisfactions of virtue, in the broadest sense of virtue, and perhaps to pity the man who could not enjoy them. And when he said that goodness brings wealth and every other blessing, he did not mean that if you behave yourself, you will get rich quick. In this context – in which he was more concerned to deny that wealth will automatically bring goodness than to persuade anyone of exactly the reverse – he was holding up a picture of the best sort of human life, in which all good things are pursued and enjoyed to the full, thanks to the exercise of practical wisdom and the other virtues.

This is indeed no ordinary set of dogmas; in fact, they are not dogmas at all. What I have called Socrates' theory of human life is not something which he explicitly expounded as such. These ideas are the ones on which he depended in his questioning of others, or which had apparently withstood trial by dialectical ordeal. The final goal, which perhaps would never be reached, was to achieve a sort of expert knowledge like the expert knowledge of skilled craftsmen, though not about shoemaking or metalwork but about the ultimate craft of living well.

What Socrates came out with in discussions should often be seen as nothing more definite than faltering steps on this road to expert moral knowledge. Sometimes the road twisted as he coaxed and prodded with irony, or tossed in an argument that seemed likely to propel his fellow-travellers in an interesting direction (or at least to make them stop and think). The result, as Nietzsche said, was wisdom full of pranks. And because it was a specifically moral sort of wisdom or knowledge that Socrates was trying to arrive at, his arguments are tinged with exhortation, idealism and appeals to the moral sentiments as well as to logic and common sense. That is why, considered in the abstract and as attempts at pure logic, they seem to have many implausible gaps of the sort Aristotle noticed.

Socrates does not just paint an inspiring picture of the ideal life. His style of talk makes an intimate marriage between exhortation and logic, which is why it stands as a contribution to argumentative philosophy rather than to preaching. Everything he says is presented in the context of an argument: reasons are demanded, inferences are examined, definitions are refined, consequences are deduced, hypotheses are rejected. This is the only approach serious enough to do justice to the matter of how one should live. Responsible exhortation must, for Socrates, be embedded in reasoned argument. A bare summary of his provisional conclusions, such as I have given here, cannot convey the strength of this marriage of idealism and down-to-earth logic. Such a summary inevitably reduces his thoughts to a shoal of beached propositions gasping out of their element. His thoughts flourished in the swim of discussion, and can be seen alive nowadays only in the setting of Plato's early dialogues.

Socrates was not an easy guru to follow, not least because a guru was one thing that he resolutely refused to be. Still, it is hardly surprising that after his death several of his friends wanted to carry on the good work somehow. Since it was, and is, no simple matter to say exactly what the good work amounted to, it should be equally unsurprising that these would-be successors of Socrates ended up championing very different causes. The greatest of his heirs was Plato. The rest were a mixed bunch. But three of them seem to have had a significant influence in one way or another.

Two of the men who were with Socrates when he died – Antisthenes of Athens, and Euclides of nearby Megara – went on to become founders or father figures of schools of thought whose traces could still be seen hundreds of years later. The school founded by a third companion of Socrates, Aristippus of Cyrene in Libya (c.435–c.355 BC), has not lived on in the same way, which was no great loss. What Aristippus and his followers made of the teachings of Socrates is of interest mainly as an instance of how easily Socrates' followers could exaggerate and twist what they had learned.

The Cyrenaics who followed Aristippus were devoted to pleasure, but in a curiously philosophical way. Impressed by the rational self-control of Socrates, Aristippus turned his own self-discipline to the single-minded pursuit of gratification. While Socrates saw no reason not to enjoy the good things in life – provided, of course, that this did not interfere with his search for virtue – Aristippus saw little reason to do anything else. After Socrates died, Aristippus became a sort of licensed court jester to Dionysius I, the tyrannical ruler of Syracuse in Sicily, who is reputed to have died in a drinking bout to celebrate winning the prize in a drama contest.

The basis of Aristippus' pursuit of enjoyment, riotous or otherwise, was apparently sincere and partly Socratic. Like most moralists, Socrates held that one must beware of becoming a slave to one's desires. Aristippus agreed. But his rather novel interpretation of this was to exert authority over his desires by getting them to work overtime for him. This made him happy; and what, after all, could be wrong with happiness? Had not Socrates dangled the promise of happiness as an incentive to virtue? There could not be much wrong with it, then.

Socrates had a somewhat highfaluting conception of happiness as a state of spiritual satisfaction obtained by noble living. Here Aristippus begged to differ. According to him, the form of happiness one should aim for was one's own physical pleasure. He regarded such pleasure as the only workable criterion of what is good and bad generally. He apparently held that it is impossible to have certain knowledge of anything but one's own sensations, a philosophical idea that had several defenders at the time. So pleasurable sensations, which were undoubtedly a good thing in some sense even if nothing else was, may have seemed the logical thing for a philosopher to concentrate on in an uncertain world.

The pursuit of pleasure was thus a serious business. The philosopher's job was to engineer his desires and his circumstances in such a way as to maximize his pleasurable sensations, and to preach the wisdom of this way of life to others (who naturally ought to pay for such valuable advice). It took the self-discipline of a Socrates to do this difficult job properly, or so Aristippus seems to have thought, and it was important not to be distracted by other pursuits that might divert one from the only practical and intelligible quest in life, namely pleasure. Mathematics and science, for example, were no help and so should be ignored. Here once more the example of Socrates could be invoked, after a fashion, for did he not relentlessly pursue the matter of how to live, at the expense of all other questions?

Socrates would have enjoyed showing Aristippus and other Cyrenaics where they had gone wrong. He would have wanted to know, for instance, what had happened to justice and the other virtues he had championed. He would also have rejected the ideas of the Cynics, though they were much more interesting. Like the Cyrenaics, Antisthenes (c.445–c.360 BC) and the later Cynics hijacked some of what they had got from Socrates and blew it out of proportion. 'A Socrates gone mad' is how Plato is supposed to have described the Cynic Diogenes, a follower of Antisthenes. But the Cynics still managed to keep more of their Socratic inheritance than did Aristippus, and indeed their main doctrine was the exact opposite of Cyrenaic indulgence.

Like Aristippus, Antisthenes thought that a Socratic strength of mind was needed for the pursuit of happiness. There the similarity with Aristippus ended. Antisthenes held that happiness was to be found not in satisfying desires, as the Cyrenaics maintained, but in losing them. He was impressed by Socrates' indifference to wealth and comfort, and turned this into an ascetic philosophy that positively embraced poverty. Socrates, after all, had said that nothing could harm a good man. Antisthenes drew the conclusion that so long as one was good, nothing else in life mattered at all. This certainly goes beyond Socrates, who never denied that wealth or possessions were, in their proper place, a better thing to have than to lack. His apparent indifference to them was largely a by-product of the demanding search for virtue and a healthy soul, not to mention mere absent-mindedness.

While Socrates was quite prepared to ignore ordinary ways and values when his principles demanded it, Antisthenes appeared to pursue unconventionality for its own sake. If something was neither virtuous nor wicked, then it did not make the slightest difference whether one did it or not. As can be imagined, this was a powerful recipe for eccentricity. Freed of the desire for possessions, and liberated from conventional behaviour, the wise man could wander around declaiming against society's foolish ways and generally making a spectacle of himself. He would console himself with the knowledge that conventional values are worthless and quite different from the natural values of the genuinely good life. Unfortunately, it was never made clear what natural values and true virtue actually involved. Antisthenes was much better at loudly saying what they were not.

Diogenes of Sinope, on the Black Sea (*c*.400–*c*.325 BC) came to Athens and was taken by the ideas of Antisthenes. But he thought that Antisthenes had failed to live up to his own teachings, which would not have been surprising. Diogenes made up for this magnificently, especially in eccentricity and unconventional living. One of the best-known tales about early philosophers says that Diogenes lived in an earthenware tub; another says that he set a fashion among the Cynics for public masturbation. True or not, the scores of stories about his wacky words and deeds show what a disconcerting impression he made. He revelled in the nickname of 'the dog' (*kyon*), which is how the Cynics, or 'dog-men', got their name. It was given to him because he sought the uncomplicated, instinctive and shameless life of an animal – animals being the true exponents of 'natural' values. He had a sharp tongue and was quick to savage those he disagreed with, which may also have contributed to his nickname. He was particularly hostile to Plato and liked to play practical jokes on him. He apparently turned up at one of Plato's lectures brandishing a plucked chicken in order to heckle him contemptuously on a point of definition – a low-life echo of Socrates' 'wisdom full of pranks'.

Diogenes' disturbing renunciation of conventional life evidently did not go so far as to make a hermit of this 'Socrates gone mad'. Life was too busy for that. There were people to be persuaded, examples to be set, there was preaching to be done and practical advice to be given. His activities seem to have made him quite popular. When his tub was destroyed, the citizens of Athens are said to have clubbed together and bought him a new one. His sincerity and the simplicity of his life seem to have been respectfully admired from a safe distance, although his teachings were far too radical to attract more than a small number of committed followers or to have any direct political effect. He taught that happiness consisted in satisfying only the most basic needs and in disciplining oneself not to want any more. Everything else was to be renounced – riches, comfort, ordinary family life – because none of it made one a morally better person. All the restrictive trappings of civilization in the city-state, from taboos against incest or eating human flesh to the institution of marriage, social-class barriers and traditional religion, were to be overcome for the same reason. The ideal society would be a loose community of spartan, self-sufficient, rational beings who indulged in any and every form of relationship to which all parties consented, unbound by conventional prohibitions.

Much of what Diogenes said was meant to shock; he probably did not make a regular habit of breaking all the taboos he condemned. But he did not want to jolt people into examining their lives. Over the years, and especially in the first two centuries of the Christian era, Cynicism attracted all sorts of wandering hippies and free-loving, back-packing beggars, who were keener on general denunciation and on ridiculing society than on philosophy or doing good. Such people, and the satirical and sarcastic literature that was influenced by the movement, gave rise to the modern meaning of 'cynical'. But the earliest Cynics, Bohemian though they were, earnestly saw themselves as moral teachers and seem to have performed a useful service. Crates of Thebes (c.365–c.285 BC), for example, gave away his sizeable fortune to become a pupil of Diogenes. He apparently made house calls as a sort of therapist or pastor, offering a service of moral guidance that was not available to ordinary people from any other source – certainly not from the formal schools of philosophical research set up by Plato and Aristotle. Hipparchia, the sister of a pupil of Crates, was desperate to join Crates in his unconventional life, but had to threaten her well-off parents with suicide before they would let her go. They eventually consented, and she 'travelled around with her husband and had intercourse publicly and went out to dinners'.

Euclides, the last of the followers of Socrates to be considered here, was so devoted to the master that when

Athens banned the citizens of Megara from entering the city, he is said to have dressed up in women's clothes and slunk in under cover of darkness to be with him. Euclides shared not only Socrates' interest in the nature of moral goodness but also his passion for argument. While Socrates often seemed prepared to follow a promising line of reasoning wherever it led to, Euclides was interested in logical arguments for their own sake, especially paradoxical ones. One opponent spoke of 'wrangling Euclides, who inspired the Megarians with a frenzied love of controversy'.

Frenzied or not, the intellectual curiosity of the Megarians led them to come up with some of the most enduring riddles about logic and language. Eubulides, a pupil of Euclides, is credited with several, including the most famous one, commonly known as the Liar. This is the paradox presented by someone who says, 'This statement is false.' The problem is what to say about such a statement; arguments about its truth tend to go round in a dizzying circle. For example, if it is false, then the speaker spoke truly because that is what he said it was. On the other hand, if he spoke truly, then it must be false because what he said is that it was false. Thus if it is false, it follows that it is true; and if it is true, it follows that it is false. This riddle is easier to make fun of than it is to solve. It has a remarkable ability to bounce back in the face of any proposed solution. One can sympathize with the poet Philetas of Cos, who is said to have worried about it so much that he wasted away, becoming so thin that he had to put lead weights in his shoes to stop himself blowing over. The epitaph on his gravestone read:

> O Stranger: Philetas of Cos am I,
> 'Twas the Liar who made me die,
> And the bad nights caused thereby.

It may be hard to see the puzzle itself as profound, but attempts to get to the bottom of it certainly have been. The Liar has stimulated a great deal of work on the nature of truth and linguistic meaning, by mathematical logicians and by linguists who look at the formal structure of languages. It seems, however, to have caused no further casualties. One eventual by-product of an interest in the sort of 'self-reference' involved in the paradox – the paradoxical statement is curiously about itself – was Gödel's Theorem, one of the most significant results of modern mathematics, which shows that there are certain limits to mathematical proof.

The pupils and successors of Euclides turned Megara into a real-life version of the farcically exaggerated 'logic factory' portrayed in Aristophanes' play about Socrates. The fact that to some sceptics their work seemed like mere 'wrangling' and controversy for its own sake, which no doubt some of it was, recalls the reception that Socrates' incessant arguments about virtue got from some of the less intellectual citizens of Athens. One reason why Euclides would have felt it was his task as a philosopher both to hold forth about moral goodness and to get involved in abstruse logical questions was his admiration for Socrates' view that knowledge is the path to virtue. Socrates may not himself have discussed logic, but Euclides probably felt that doing so was one way to continue the search for wisdom. In particular, if one understood the process of argument, then this would presumably help one to carry on the good work of Socratic examination.

All these schools of philosophy that flowed from Socrates shared his idea that wisdom brings virtue and virtue brings happiness. They evidently differed over what they took happiness to involve – indulgent pleasure in the case of the Cyrenaics, ascetic discipline in the case of the Cynics. But they agreed that philosophical reflection of some sort was the way to find it, and that such an occupation amounted to the good life. The ethical views of these philosophers were all rather individualistic (to an extreme, in the case of Diogenes) and one can see how the unusual example of Socrates' life could have led to this. But in the case of the Cynics, at least, there was a clear break with Socrates over the ties of social obligation and about loyalty to the values of the city-state. The Cynics stressed a contrast between the life of virtue and the life enjoined by the city in which one happens to be born or live. In one sense Socrates did this too, but in another sense he did not. He certainly would have accepted that the individual must follow his own conscience, not the city's dictates when those dictates are unjust. But he sought to better the life of the city, not to relinquish it altogether. He urged the Athenians to live justly together and to improve their laws and behaviour where necessary, not to abandon the whole enterprise of civilization and lose respect for the law.

Socrates made it clear that although you must disobey the laws if they are unjust, you must nevertheless submit to punishment if caught, which is exactly what he himself did when he was condemned. Some friends gave him the chance to escape prison and flee Athens before execution; one of Plato's early dialogues, the *Crito*, deals with this episode and gives Socrates' reasons for rejecting the offer. As well as feeling a moral obligation to the legitimate authority of the city and the due process of law, Socrates loved Athens and did not relish life anywhere else. Some of the things he is made to say in Plato's dialogues suggest that he had misgivings about democracy as a form of government; this has led to him being sometimes described as anti-democratic. But it was really Plato who had those misgivings, as he did eventually about all the forms of government he came across. Socrates himself showed every sign of deep loyalty to the constitution of Athens. He often praised the city and its institutions, and seems never to have left it except on its military service. On the question of whether he approved its type of democracy, Socrates voted with his feet – or rather, showed his preference by failing to do so. There were many other states with non-democratic governments to which he could have emigrated. Perhaps most embarrassingly for those of his opponents in his own time who would have liked to cast him as an enemy of democracy, it was well known that he had risked death under the anti-democratic Tyrants by refusing to take part in the arrest of an innocent man.

Socrates was, if anything, too democratic for the Athenians. It was this aspect of his character and teaching which led to the exaggerated individualism of some of his imitators. His attitude to religion and morality can be seen as ultra-democratic. Nothing is to be taken for granted, especially not if it is handed down by an authority which puts itself above the moral reasoning of the people, be that putative authority in the form of Zeus or of a human tyrant. Every man must work out for himself what is good and right, and nobody can escape the obligation of examining himself and his life. The result of such discussions between citizens should ideally be a just society with just laws, arrived at through such collective self-examination. In the Socratic dream of democracy, individual conviction would lead to collective agreement – not about everything, presumably, but at least about the outlines of how to live.

Socrates was no politician. He felt he could play his part only by debating with individuals, one by one or in small groups: 'I know how to produce one witness to the truth of what I say, the man with whom I am debating, but the others I ignore. I know how to secure one man's vote, but with the many I will not even enter into discussion.'

Over the years, the votes for Socrates have steadily accumulated as Plato's dialogues have carried his debating, or a semblance of it, far beyond fifth-century Athens and its dinner parties. There are now at any rate few who would disagree with one thing that Socrates told his judges: 'If you put me to death, you will not easily find anyone to take my place.'

SOURCES

Abbreviations used in these notes:

CDP *The Collected Dialogues of Plato*, E. Hamilton and H. Cairns (eds) (Princeton University Press, 1961)

CWA *The Collected Works of Aristotle*, J. Barnes (ed.) (Princeton University Press, 1984)

LCL Loeb Classical Library

LOP *Lives of the Philosophers*, Diogenes Laertius, translated by R. D. Hicks (Harvard University Press, 1972)

p. 3 You are mistaken ... Plato, *Apology*, 28b (CDP, p. 14)

p. 3–4 started wrestling ... Plato, *Symposium*, 220c (CDP, p. 571)

p. 4 fell into a fit ... ibid., 174d, 175b (CDP, pp. 529–30)

p. 4 I have never lived ... Plato, *Apology*, 36b (CDP, p. 21)

p. 5 anyone who is close ... Plato, *Laches*, 187e (CDP, p. 131)

p. 5 Marsyas: Plato, *Symposium*, 215b (CDP, p. 566)

p. 5–6 speaking for myself ... ibid., 215d (CDP, p. 567)

p. 6 I've been bitten ... ibid., 218a (CDP, p. 569)

p. 7–8 The first step, then ... Xenophon, *The Banquet*, V (transl. adapted from E. C. Marchant and O. J. Todd, Xenophon, LCL edn, 1923, Vol. 4, p. 599)

p. 14 After puzzling about it ... Plato, *Apology*, 21b (CDP, p. 7)

p. 14 I reflected as I walked away ... ibid., 21d (CDP, p. 7)

p. 14–15 whenever I succeed ... ibid., 23a (CDP, p. 9)

p. 15 the arguments never ... Plato, *Theaetetus*, 161a (CDP, p. 866)

p. 15–16 If I say that this ... Plato, *Apology*, 37e (CDP, p. 23)

p. 16 it has always been ... Plato, *Crito*, 46b (CDP, p. 31)

p. 16 in obedience to God's commands ... Plato, *Apology*, 33c (CDP, p. 19)

p. 17 I want you to think ... ibid., 22a (CDP, p. 8)

p. 17 when it comes ... ibid., 31d (CDP, p. 17)

p. 18 I spend all my time ... ibid., 30a (CDP, p. 16)

p. 18 ashamed that you give ... ibid., 29e (CDP, p. 16)

p. 18 these people give you ... ibid., 36e (CDP, p. 22)

p. 19 Apollodorus: Xenophon, *Socrates' Defence*, 28

p. 19 to be afraid of death ... Plato, *Apology*, 29a (CDP, p. 15)

p. 19 heroes of the old days, ibid., 41b (CDP, p. 25)

p. 20 the work of ... Plato, *2nd Letter*, 314c (CDP, p. 1,567)

p. 21 All his private conduct ... Xenophon, *Memoirs of Socrates*, IV (transl. E. C. Marchant, LCL edn, p. 309)

p. 21 old prig ... Jonathan Barnes, *The Presocratic Philosophers* (Routledge, 1982), p.448

p. 22 modern scholars: particularly Gregory Vlastos, *Socrates: Ironist and Moral Philosopher* (Cambridge, 1991); *Socratic Studies* (Cambridge, 1994)

p. 23 purified, (etc.): Plato, *Phaedo*, 67c–d (CDP, p. 50)

p. 25 mathematics has come to be ... Aristotle, *Metaphysics*, 992a32 (CWA, p. 1568)

p.26 our birth is but a sleep ... Wordsworth, *Intimations of Immortality* V, (1807)

p.27 we have helped him ... Plato, *Meno*, 84b (CDP, p. 368)

p. 28 At present these opinions ... ibid., 85c (CDP, p. 370)

p. 28 I shall question him ... Plato, *Apology*, 29e (CDP, p. 16)

p. 29 sometimes, however ... Plato, *Lesser Hippias*, 372d (CDP, p. 209)

p. 29 I am full of defects ... ibid., 372b (CDP, p. 209)

p. 30 an accurate knowledge ... Plato, *Euthyphro*, 5a (CDP, p. 172)

p. 31 is what is holy ... ibid., 10a (CDP, p. 178)

p. 32 Those who believe that God ... Leibniz, *Theodicy* (1710), 176 (transl. E. M. Huggard, Open Court, 1985, p. 236)

p. 33 We must not limit our enquiry ... Aristotle, *Magna Moralia*, 1182a4 (CWA, p. 1868)

p. 33 he thought all the virtues ... ibid., 1216b2 (adapted from CWA, p. 1925)

p. 34 he is doing away with ... ibid., 1182a21 (CWA, p. 1868)

p. 34 No one, he said, acts ... Aristotle, *Nicomachean Ethics*, 1145b27 (CWA, p. 1810)

p. 35 in the strength of his character ... K. Joel, in W. K. C. Guthrie, *Socrates* (Cambridge, 1971), p. 138

p. 36 Milton: *Paradise Lost*, IV. 110

p. 36 no one would choose evil ... Aristotle, *Magna Moralia*, 1200b26 (CWA, p. 1900)

p. 36 divine naiveté ... Nietzsche, *The Birth of Tragedy* (1872), 13 (transl. W. Kaufmann, Random House, 1967, p. 88)

p. 36 wisdom full of pranks: Nietzsche, *Der Wanderer und sein Schatten* (1880), 86

p. 36 This was Socrates' ... Galen, *On the Use of the Parts of the Body*, I.9

p. 37 mutilated by ... Plato, *Crito*, 47e (CDP, p. 33)

p. 37 nothing can harm ... Plato, *Apology*, 41d (CDP, p. 25)

p. 37 the difficulty is not ... ibid., 39b (CDP, p.24)

p. 38 to live well means ... Plato, *Crito*, 48b (CDP, p. 33)

p. 38 the just is happy ... Plato, *Republic*, 354a (CDP, p. 604)

p.40 –41 So there is every ... Plato, *Gorgias*, 507b (CDP, p. 289)

p. 41 Those who say that the victim ... Aristotle, *Nicomachean Ethics*, 1153b19 (CWA, p. 1823)

p. 41 if you are serious ... Plato, *Gorgias*, 481c (CDP, p. 265)

p. 41 it is no ordinary matter ... Plato, *Republic*, 352d

p. 46 A Socrates gone mad: Diogenes Laertius, *Lives of the Philosophers*, VI.54 (LOP, Vol. 2, p. 55)

p. 49 travelled around with her husband ... *Lives of the Philosophers*, VI.96 (as transl. J. M. Rist in *Stoic Philosophy*, Cambridge, 1969, p. 61)

p. 50 wrangling Euclides ... Timon of Phlius, in Diogenes Laertius, op. cit., II.107 (LOP, Vol.1, p. 237)

p. 51 O Stranger ... Athenaeus, *Deipnosophistai*, IX.410E (transl. St George Stock in *Stoicism*, London, 1908, p. 36)

p. 51 Gödel's Theorem: see *Gödel's Proof*, E. Nagel and J. R. Newman (London, 1959)

p. 54 I know how to produce ... Plato, *Gorgias*, 474a (CDP, p. 256)

p. 54 If you put me to death ... Plato, *Apology*, 30e (CDP, p. 16)